# Hats On Heads

written by Pam Holden

A fireman has a
hat like this one.

A cowboy has a
hat like this one.

A cook has a hat like this one.

A policeman has a
hat like this one.

A swimmer has a
hat like this one.

A coach has a
hat like this one.

A beekeeper has a hat like this one.

A clown has a hat
like this one.